D0983070

THE CRITICISM OF T. S. ELIOT
Problems of an "Impersonal Theory" of Poetry

Undergraduate Prize Essays: Yale University

VOLUME VII

*This essay is published for the
Committee on Undergraduate Prize Essays
upon the Hadley Fund.*

THE CRITICISM OF T. S. ELIOT

Problems of an "Impersonal Theory"
of Poetry

BY

VICTOR H. BROMBERT

Class of 1947 M

New Haven · Yale University Press
London · Geoffrey Cumberlege · Oxford University Press
1949

The Printing-Office of the Yale University Press

ACKNOWLEDGMENTS

I wish to express my gratitude to Professor W. K. Wimsatt of Yale University for his patient guidance and careful criticism during the writing of this essay. His knowledge of the subject and his sharp insight into problems of literary criticism were a great stimulus to me.

I also wish to thank Mr. C. Beecher Hogan for his very helpful suggestions and Professor Thomas W. Copeland for the invaluable assistance given me in preparing this manuscript for publication.

VICTOR H. BROMBERT

Yale University
April, 1949

I

Honest criticism and sensitive
appreciation are directed not
upon the poet but upon poetry.

"Tradition and the Individual Talent"

WHAT Eliot himself calls his "impersonal theory of poetry"
is first mentioned by name in his early essay "Tradition
and the Individual Talent."[1] This essay does not provide a
full exploration of the theory, but it contains many statements from
which important deductions can be drawn. Perhaps the most noteworthy of these statements is Eliot's comment on the appreciation of
art:

The effect of a work of art upon the person who enjoys it is an experience different in kind from any experience not of art.

Clearly this short sentence suggests a definite attitude toward literature.
In the light of Eliot's subsequent development, it even constitutes a
fundamental commitment. Since this commitment may well be a key
to Eliot's entire position as a critic, it is important that we understand
some of its implications.

Any impersonal theory of literature, while granting that a number of
uses may legitimately be made of literary works, insists on making the
distinction between minor uses—or what might be called by-products
—and the major use which consists of an appreciation of intrinsic values.
The nature of this major use will perhaps become clearer if we first
briefly examine the various uses which the apostle of an impersonal
theory would be careful to relegate to a position of secondary importance.

In the first place, literature may be used as a document, that is, as
evidence concerning the social and ideological background of a particular work, or as pertinent data concerning the psychology of the
author. Frequently, for instance, we expect the literary artist to give us
a picture of a certain society or to describe a chain of historical events.
When we make those demands on an author, we use his work as a

1. First published in two separate parts in the *Egoist,* VI (Sept.–Oct., Nov.–Dec., 1919).

document of social or political history. We call on Meredith and Dickens for a glimpse at the Victorian age; we expect to learn something about the Chinese revolution from *Man's Fate;* we hope to discover in Pushkin a mirror of the Russian nobility—only to find out later that as documents these works were either distorted by the creative imagination of the artist or that they added nothing new to already available sources of information.

Again, if the writer has in some way expressed abstract thoughts or philosophic beliefs, the reader may turn to his works for the sake of studying his ideas. When thus used, literature is transformed into a philosophical or ideological document. According to Eliot such a use is particularly dangerous and indicates an inability to distinguish between two fundamentally different activities: that of the poet and that of the philosopher.[2]

Very frequently, also, we use a poem as a personal document, a revelation of the mood, feelings, and state of mind of an individual whose personality seems interesting or attractive to us. We use a poem as a lens or microscope through which we can observe the inner workings of a mind. But when the poem is thus used as a psychological document, we show greater interest in the poet than in the poem. Eliot considers this type of use particularly misleading since, as he suggests in "Tradition and the Individual Talent," "the poet has, not a 'personality' to express, but a particular medium, which is only a medium and not a personality . . ."[3] F. O. Mathiessen, whose critical thought frequently echoes the thought of Eliot, insists that by reducing the poem to a document "you lose all contact with the experience that a work of art exists to communicate," and he explains that a work of art is not a document since "it possesses in a very real sense a life of its own which is distinct from the biography of its creator and also from any idea or belief that it expresses."[4] This is precisely what Eliot means in "Tradi-

2. "I believe that for a poet to be also a philosopher he would have to be virtually two men; I cannot think of any example of this thorough schizophrenia, nor can I see anything to be gained by it: the work is better performed inside two skulls than one." *The Use of Poetry and the Use of Criticism,* p. 90.

3. In such early essays as "Tradition and the Individual Talent," Eliot's attitude is often uncompromising. I refer in particular to his comparison of the mind of the poet to a shred of platinum. According to this analogy, the mind of the poet is merely a catalyst. J. C. Ransom, in *The New Criticism,* remarks that this analogy does not identify the chemicals in the reaction and suggests, moreover, that it leads to a doctrine of "poetic automatism." Eliot himself has later repudiated this analogy in *After Strange Gods* (1933), although on the whole he still upheld the ideas expressed in "Tradition and the Individual Talent."

4. F. O. Mathiessen, *The Achievement of T. S. Eliot,* pp. 113, 128.

tion and the Individual Talent" when he says that art can give us an experience unlike any other experience that is not of art.

Not uncommonly literature is also used as a tool for a wide range of practical purposes, as an influential instrument in education, or even for the propagation of social and political ideas. Thus we hear about art the civilizer, art the educator, art the propagandist, art the moralist. Eliot agrees that art may serve a variety of purposes, but he maintains that this by no means constitutes the proper function of art. "I do not deny that art may be affirmed to serve ends beyond itself; but art is not required to be aware of these ends . . ." he writes a few years later in "The Function of Criticism,"[5] adding, with proper emphasis on the autotelic nature of art, that it performs its function much better by indifference to these ends. For just as a poem cannot be a substitute for thought, philosophy, or theology, so these cannot be substitutes for a poem.[6] According to the impersonal theory, a work of art not only gives the person who enjoys it an experience quite different from any experience that is not of art but it is also an end in itself which need be justified neither in terms of its intent nor in those of its effect.

No literary work, of course, can exist in a vacuum. But neither the experience leading up to the creation of the poem nor its effect on the reader can give us an indication about its nature as a work of art. In his Harvard lectures in 1932–33, Eliot very aptly distinguished the various "experiences," all of which exist but none of which constitutes the work of art: "What the poet experienced is not poetry but poetic material; the writing of the poetry is a fresh experience for him, and the reading of it, by the author or by anyone else, is another thing still."[7] By this token "what a poem means is as much what it means to others as what it means to the author."[8] Some people might object in this manner: But surely it is the function of the artist to communicate a personal feeling and make us share it. If the poem can mean something to the author and something else to the reader, is that not a sign of its failure? Moreover, is it not the function of the poet to "exteriorize" the poetic materials he experienced? Now all this is true, but it is true only if we consider the poem as a personal document. The central question is whether it be the artist's function to *communicate* or rather,

5. First published in the *Criterion*, II (Oct., 1923). This essay is, in Eliot's own words, "an application of the principles expressed in 'Tradition and the Individual Talent.'"
6. This idea was taken up again in "Experiment and Criticism," *The Bookman* (Nov., 1929) and in "Poetry and Propaganda," *The Bookman* (Feb., 1930).
7. *The Use of Poetry and the Use of Criticism*, p. 118.
8. *Ibid.*, p. 122.

as Eliot suggests, *to write poetry*. According to the impersonal theory
of poetry, the original experience, in the process of artistic creation, is
inevitably transformed into something different and frequently quite
unrecognizable. For after all, what is this experience which is to be
communicated? "By the time it has settled down into a poem it may
be so different from the original experience as to be hardly recogniz-
able. The 'experience' in question may be a result of a fusion of feelings
so numerous, and ultimately so obscure in their origins, that even if
there be communication of them, the poet may hardly be aware of
what he is communicating; and what is there to be communicated was
not in existence before the poem was completed."[9] It is the last statement in this passage which appears to me as the most significant: what
is in the poem was not there before it was completed. This means that
if we wish at all to discuss poetry in terms of communication, we have
to consider the poem both as the communicating vehicle and the thing
to be communicated. Eliot emphasizes not only that the *intent* and the
effect are not the poem but also that what the poem *is* is something new,
something that stands apart both from the creator and from the material
used for the creation. This is only another way of saying that "the
difference between art and the event is always absolute."[10] In the
process of creation, the author's personality, to use a phrase of James
Joyce, is "refined out of existence."[11] And the real existence of the completed work of art, according to Eliot, is neither in the artist's nor in
the reader's feelings but somewhere in between the reader and the
artist. The work of art has become "public property," as it were, and
must be considered on its own merits.

But what about Eliot's conception of literary criticism? On the basis
of his attitude toward the appreciation of literature, what logical deductions follow about the nature and function of the literary critic? So
far we have examined his belief in the autotelic nature of art which

9. *Ibid.*, p. 131.
10. "Tradition and the Individual Talent." In other words, the emotion we have for
the artistic object is not the same as the emotion we have for the natural object. J. C.
Ransom, who likes to translate Eliot into his own terms, calls this the difference between
the *practical* and the *speculative* emotion. See *The New Criticism*. I. A. Richards makes a
somewhat similar distinction when he claims that an "actual murder" leads the witness
to "overt action," whereas a "theatrical presentation of a murder" only leads the audience
to "imaginal" or "incipient action." See *Principles of Literary Criticism*, pp. 110–111.
11. *A Portrait of the Artist as a Young Man*, p. 252. In the light of this statement, it would
be interesting to compare the artistic merit of *Stephen Hero* with that of *A Portrait of the
Artist*.

developed from his original premise that appreciation, at least theoretically, is different in kind from any other nonartistic experience. But literary criticism, according to Eliot, is not an autotelic activity. This, in Eliot's opinion, constitutes a basic difference between all art and all criticism. Whereas art is not required to have any ends in view, being as it is an end in itself, criticism, as Eliot has pointed out, is by definition about something other than itself.[12] This again may appear to be a truism; and yet the distinction becomes significant if we consider for a while a category of so-called critics whom Eliot has most vigorously denounced for calling themselves "critics" while not being at all aware of this basic distinction.

Articles, essays, and books have been written with the avowed purpose of critically discussing a given work of art but which in fact only supplied the fancy or opinion of a particular individual. For some critics are more interested in their own mental and emotional responses to a work of art than in that work of art itself. They wish to interpret the poem or play according to their own sensibility or to give us an impressionistic account of their own private experience in reading it. To such critics criticism is an intensely personal affair; they all more or less subscribe to the famous dictum of Anatole France that criticism is the confession of the adventures of a man's soul among books. What we can gain from reading such "interpretations" or "impressionistic criticisms" is much more an intimate knowledge of the critic than a better understanding of the work of art that is being discussed. This has its unquestionable value: if we are interested in Stendhal's thoughts about the nature of comedy, there is something to be learned from his remarks about Molière; and certainly anyone studying Gide's theories about the art of writing a novel ought to read his lectures on Dostoevski. It is very doubtful, however, whether we can gain from either Gide or Stendhal a truer understanding of the real nature of the artistic achievements of Dostoevski or Molière. These critics are more concerned with their own ideas than with the nature of the object under discussion. Even Eliot has not been entirely guiltless of this kind of criticism: when he speaks about Baudelaire's prose writings, one has the impression of learning more about Eliot than about Baudelaire.

Criticism of this sort has its value. When we are studying the moral and intellectual temper of a certain period, we ought to investigate its opinions about the past. The Romantic conception of Greece can tell

12. "The Function of Criticism."

us much about the ethos of the nineteenth century. So a writer's opinion about another author can offer us an insight into his personality. This does not mean, however, that the original is not frequently distorted. As Eliot has pointed out, *Hamlet* as seen by Goethe and Coleridge has become more and more a creation of Goethe and Coleridge and less and less the play of Shakespeare. "For what is Coleridge's *Hamlet*," asks Eliot in "The Function of Criticism," "is it an honest inquiry as far as the data permit, or is it an attempt to present Coleridge in an attractive costume?" According to Eliot, the particular vice of English criticism is that it is more concerned with appreciation than analysis. "English criticism is inclined to argue or persuade rather than to state," he writes in one of his essays in *The Sacred Wood*.[13] And one of the reasons why Eliot has admired French criticism is that, in the main, it is analytical in its approach. Eliot is an "Aristotelian" in continually reminding us that the critic's proper business is a direct concern with the object under discussion.[14] Criticism—that is, real criticism—must not be a pretext for venting one's feelings and thoughts, no matter how interesting they may be, but a sincere attempt by means of analysis and comparison to assess the work of art according to certain standards. If we accept Eliot's assumptions and arguments, it follows that a work of art cannot be interpreted or explained, for in the process of interpretation it ceases to be what it is and becomes something new, namely the creation of the critic. And this is precisely the difference Eliot makes between criticism and art: for whereas the artist may and probably ought to be critical at the same time that he is being creative, the critic has no business being creative. To use Eliot's formula: "... you cannot fuse criticism with creation."[15] The critic must above all have a highly developed sense of fact for he is dealing primarily with a fact, namely the work of art.[16]

This does not mean that the critic should be without either sensibility or personality: on the contrary, both the personality and the sensi-

13. "Philip Massinger," *The Sacred Wood*.
14. F. O. Mathiessen, in *The Achievement of T. S. Eliot*, p. 6, remarks that there is an actual closeness in this respect between Eliot and Matthew Arnold: "For certainly there is in each a full understanding of the unremitting discipline for the critic in learning 'to see the object as it is' . . ."
15. "The Function of Criticism."
16. Eliot does not wish to replace taste or appreciation by a sense of fact. On the contrary, it seems that he sees in facts a possible protection for taste. Eliot knows, of course, that many facts are quite irrelevant. But at least fact cannot corrupt taste: "The real corrupters are those who supply opinion or fancy . . ." ("The Function of Criticism"). On the other hand, only real taste enables the critic to recognize the significant fact.

bility of the critic are highly desirable; without them, the critic can neither be appreciative of art nor forceful enough to dominate his subject and convey his findings to the reader. But sensibility and personality are to be used as tools and should at all times be subservient to the main task. The critic works through the intelligence not the emotions.

In considering the nature of an "ideal critic," Eliot suggests that, at least while performing his task, he should have no emotions except those "immediately provoked by a work of art."[17] Such an ideal critic is probably an illusion: first, because no human being can altogether successfully compartmentalize his mind; and second, because we have no reason to assume that the momentary obliteration of one's "private" emotions would not at the same time render the appreciation of a work of art quite impossible. Eliot therefore has to concede a few years later that there probably never has been and never will be a critic of any art "whose appreciation was a separate faculty, quite judicious and wholly isolated from his other interests and his private passions."[18] No matter how true this may be, Eliot nevertheless insists that it is the appreciation and not the private feeling that counts. Although an ideal cannot be reached, the concept of that ideal can give us at least a bearing and tell us what to strive for. As I. A. Richards has pointed out, there is always a difference between an ideal reader's "possible" experience and the real reader's "actual" experience.[19] But the real reader's experience can no doubt be improved if he keeps in mind the requisites for an ideal reading.

Now these conditions are the same for the critic as they are for the reader. It is true that the critic's appreciation is not a separate faculty and that in fact, although ideally he should experience only the emotions produced by the work of art, his appreciation depends on his sensibility which has been conditioned by numerous private experiences. Sensibility is a highly complex thing: it is made up of many emotions and feelings, past and present, which may be in conflict with each other. Some of these latent emotions or feelings are likely to contribute to the reader's enjoyment but others, if permitted to assert themselves, may constitute an insuperable barrier to the appreciation of a particular work. It is therefore the special and first task of the critic's intelligence to know and recognize his own emotional barriers and limitations and to approach the work of art with the utmost restraint and

17. "The Perfect Critic," *The Sacred Wood.*
18. "Poetry and Propaganda," *The Bookman,* LXX (Feb., 1930).
19. *Principles of Literary Criticism,* p. 225.

with a mind as devoid as possible of any preconceived notions.[20] All this is to signify, of course, that reason ought to be the dominating force. And, indeed, the dangers of a purely emotional approach for a critic are only too evident. These are the same dangers that the ordinary reader whose emotions are not checked by reason is likely to incur. To give an extreme example, imagine, for instance, the sort of impression that Chaucer's *Prioress' Tale* might produce on a Jew in times of persecution. Unless he was an unusually intelligent and dispassionate person, his response would most certainly be unfavorable. It would bring back to his mind not only his situation but the entire medieval myth of Jewish crucifiers and Jewish poisoners. He would condemn the poem on two counts: for the attitude of the Prioress as well as for the possible effect the tale might have on the minds of readers. And yet, no matter how legitimate his moral or emotional responses might be, he would not be judging the tale as a work of art but rather on the basis of its supposed purpose and its potential effect. To be sure, the intelligent and relatively dispassionate person might also, under the conditions mentioned above, be irritated by the poem, but at least he would understand on what grounds he preferred not to read it: he would know that he was neglecting or condemning the work of art on nonartistic grounds. He would know that what he was condemning was not the poem but its historical background.

Of course, we are free to neglect art and at times probably ought to. For each individual there are moments in his life when the enjoyment of art—even the best—becomes hardly tolerable. But whenever we approach a work of art with the sincere desire of gaining a worthwhile and pleasurable experience, we ought to understand that our private emotions are not to be permitted to interfere with the emotions produced by the work. "The end of the enjoyment of poetry is a pure contemplation from which all the accidents of personal emotion are removed."[21] The main danger of a predominantly emotional approach for a critic resides precisely in the possibility of his not seeing quite clearly *what* he is criticizing and of not being able to keep his eyes fixed on the object under discussion. The temptation to give expression to

20. I. A. Richards, whose approach is nearly always "psychological," makes very similar remarks: "Any honest reader knows fairly well the points at which his sensibility is distorted, at which he fails as a normal critic and in what ways. It is his duty to take these into consideration in passing judgment upon the value of a work. His rank as a critic depends at least as much upon his ability to discount these personal peculiarities as upon any hypothetical impeccability of his responses." *Principles of Literary Criticism,* p. 224.
21. "The Perfect Critic," *The Sacred Wood.*

his own personal response or to discuss the work of art in relation to its supposed intent and effect may be too great. It is to avoid such pitfalls that Eliot persistently emphasizes the critic's need of arduous mental discipline, thus closely echoing Charles Maurras' assertion that the critic's feelings must be at all times organized and ruled by reason, which can only be achieved if the critic possesses a *"sensibilité réfléchie."*[22] In an editorial discussion of the "modern tendency," Eliot observes with great keenness that there is a trend—and he leaves no doubt that in his opinion this is a very desirable trend—"toward a higher and clearer conception of Reason, and a more severe and serene control of the emotions by Reason."[23]

So far, in our attempt to understand Eliot's conception of the nature and function of the literary critic, we have seen that criticism, being by definition concerned with something other than itself, is not an autotelic activity; that it is therefore not to be an account of personal feeling and private response; and finally that, although sensibility and personality are required, the critic works through the intelligence and not the emotions. In an early essay published in the *Egoist*, Eliot made a few important general remarks about criticism which may well serve to sum up much of what we have already discussed:

The work of the critic is almost wholly comprehended in the "complementary activities" of comparison and analysis. The one activity implies the other; and together they provide the only way of asserting standards and of isolating a writer's peculiar merits. In the dogmatic or lazy mind comparison is supplied by judgement, analysis replaced by appreciation. Judgement and appreciation are merely tolerable avocations, no part of the critic's serious business. If the critic has performed his laboratory work well, his understanding will be evidence of appreciation; but his work is by the intelligence not the emotions. The judgement also will take place in the reader's mind, not in the critic's ex-

22. See Charles Maurras' *Prologue d'un Essai sur la Critique.* Maurras, the former editor of the royalist *Action Française,* has been an important figure among the recent French antiromantic critics. In his *Prologue* as well as in *L'Avenir de l'Intelligence,* Maurras holds that a balance between the mental and physical nature of man, with reason as the guiding force, is the primary condition for sound criticism as well as for sound art. He has also advocated the inseparability of form and content, the need for tradition, separation of "genres," and economy of expression. Ants Oras, in his essay on T. S. Eliot, gives some useful indications about the extent to which Eliot has been influenced by Maurras' ideas. Eliot himself has admitted this influence in a "Lettre d'Angleterre" published in the *Nouvelle Revue Française* (Nov., 1923): "Sauf quelques exceptions: je peux témoigner de l'importante influence qu'a eu sur mon développement intellectuel *L'Avenir de l'Intelligence* . . ." In this connection, one might also refer to Julien Benda and T. E. Hulme, both of whom Eliot has much respected, and to whose ideas he himself frequently refers.

23. "The Idea of the Literary Critic," *Criterion,* IV (Jan., 1926).

plicit statement. Where he judges or appreciates he simply . . . is missing out a link in the exposition.[24]

To what extent Eliot has practiced what he preached remains of course another question. But we must remember that the soundness and usefulness of a critic's theories cannot always be evaluated by his own practices. Nor should we be tempted, on the other hand, to discard his practical criticism because it does not seem to correspond to his theoretical position. Eliot may at times himself have succumbed to the very vices he denounced. He too may at times have "missed out a link in the exposition." But it is very doubtful whether even today Eliot would refute his early demand formulated in "The Perfect Critic" that "the critic must not coerce, and he must not make judgements for worse and better. He must simply elucidate: the reader will form the correct judgement for himself."[25]

Eliot does not deny that there exist different purposes, motives, and methods in criticism concerned with literary art. He makes this point very clear in his "Studies in Contemporary Criticism," published in the *Egoist* in 1918. But all these other forms of criticism are not "literary" criticism since they are concerned with either the intentional or the affective aspect of a poem or play, not with intrinsic value. For instance, the biographer uses the poem as a document in his researches. He may even have to be "critical" in his attempt to evaluate it as an authentic and reliable document. But he tells us nothing about the value of the poem qua poem. The same is true of the literary historian, who is concerned with literary movements, currents of ideas, and the like, and who, although he may need a sense of values as well as definite critical gifts, is not properly speaking a critic. "He must not have any very pronounced theory or scheme and must not set out to prove anything very important."[26] Such a critic of literary history, as Eliot sees it, was Sainte-Beuve. In the same essay in the *Egoist,* Eliot goes so far as to qualify this kind of criticism, which is not directly concerned with aesthetic problems, as dissociative and destructive. We may not wish to go all the way with Eliot in calling Sainte-Beuve's criticism dissociative or destructive. In many respects it is very far from being that. And yet, such were the variety of his interests and the breadth of his understanding that the resulting "tolerance" makes much of Sainte-Beuve's criticism seem invertebrate. When everything can be explained

24. "Studies in Contemporary Criticism" (1), *Egoist,* V (Oct., 1918).
25. "The Perfect Critic," *The Sacred Wood.*
26. "Beyle and Balzac," *Athenaeum* (May, 1919).

in terms of milieu and historical development, standards and value judgments tend to disappear. "After such knowledge, what forgiveness?" asks the old man, Gerontion, who also knew too much.[27]

As to the moralist and the psychologist, their concern lies with the effect upon the audience and the psychological responses of the reader rather than with the work of art itself. Here again we learn little or nothing about the intrinsic value of the art product. Of course a poem may—and usually does—deal with an ethical situation. But as J. C. Ransom has pointed out in "Criticism as Pure Speculation,"[28] "the poetic consideration of the ethical situation is not the same as the ethical consideration of it." Art, according to both Eliot and Ransom, is in fact postethical rather than ethical.

The literary critic, Eliot believes, must not be philosophizing about art; nor is he concerned with the genetic aspect of the artistic activity. As for the "social function" or purpose of a work of art as well as its possible effects on the nerves of the audience—these matters all lie outside of his domain. All of these various inquiries are of course perfectly legitimate, but in Eliot's opinion every inquirer ought to know exactly what he is doing and may legitimately fulfill only one function or, if he is unusually gifted, several, but *without confusion*. It is imperative, then, that the critic, explicitly or implicitly, indicate his standards as well as the standpoint from which he chooses to discuss whatever he is discussing.

The literary critic, if he is to follow Eliot's advice, should be concerned with that character of literature by which it "exists" somewhere between the artist and the reader. He has his own field, no matter how difficult it may be to mark its boundaries, and ought to be aware whenever he is trespassing on someone else's domain. Some people might object here by remarking first that, after all, neither art nor criticism can be thus isolated, and secondly that, even if it could be done, much would be lost in appreciation and understanding.

The first objection is easily overcome if we remember that Eliot does

27. Eliot's paradoxical belief that an individual can have too much knowledge for his own good appears again in quite different context in his remarks about "The Humanism of Irving Babbitt," *Forum*, 80 (1928): "Professor Babbitt knows too much; and by that I do not mean merely erudition or information or scholarship. I mean that he knows too many religions and philosophies, has assimilated their spirit too thoroughly (there is probably no one in England or America who understands early Buddhism better than he) to be able to give himself to any."

28. This essay was part of a symposium of critical essays, *The Intent of the Critic*, D. A. Stauffer, ed., pp. 65–88.

not ask for isolation but merely for order: the literary critic is not a substitute for the moralist or the theologian, though he should understand
that his work may lead to other fields of studies and that his activities
border on other domains. Eliot agrees that the literary critic is not
merely a literary critic just as the artist is not merely an artist. In both
cases, it is the "whole man" who is engaged in a very specialized activity. Eliot is consequently justified in stating that in all probability
"the possession of clear literary standards must imply the possession of
clear moral standards."[29] But this statement in no way contradicts Eliot's
earlier assertion that ". . . an interest in morals will not produce sound
criticism of art."[30]

As to the second and more serious objection, namely that a concern
with the intent or the effect of a work of art may increase appreciation
and understanding, we may be inclined to agree. But immediately the
question arises whether this appreciation and understanding be not of
something outside of the work of art itself. Professor Lowes' exhaustive
Road to Xanadu serves as a good example. Based on documentary proof,
this work is a fascinating study of Coleridge's "poetic material" (at
least such material as he gathered from his enormous reading), of its
accumulation in the "unconscious well" of his memory, and finally
of its transformation in the process of the artistic creation of *Kubla Khan*
and *The Rime of the Ancient Mariner*. Professor Lowes indeed succeeds
in demonstrating that "every great imaginative conception is a vortex
into which everything under the sun may be swept," and he reaches
the conclusion that the Well, the Vision, and the Will are the three
necessary factors in the imaginative process. It remains doubtful, however, whether this painstaking study, in spite of its very real interest,
contributes in any way to our enjoyment of the two great poems
beyond the pleasure we may obtain from observing a genial mind at
work or from recognizing that such or such an image has been bor-
rowed from a certain travel book of the period. The matter has thus
been summed up by Eliot: "I prefer not to define, or test, poetry by
means of speculation about its origins; you cannot find a sure test for
poetry, a test by which you may distinguish between poetry and mere
good verse, by reference to its putative antecedents in the mind of the
poet."[31] And what is literary criticism if not, at the very basis, just this
attempt to distinguish the genuine from the sham, real poetry from

29. "Experiment in Criticism," *The Bookman*, LXX (Nov., 1929).
30. "The Local Flavour," *Athenaeum* (Dec. 12, 1919).
31. *The Use of Poetry and the Use of Criticism*, p. 132.

mere good verse? And the reason why Eliot believes we cannot find a sure test for poetry by means of speculations about its intent is—as has been pointed out again more recently by W. K. Wimsatt and M. C. Beardsley[32]—that design may be a cause but cannot be a standard for judging the value of a poem as poetry and that indeed the only way the value of a poem can be measured and assessed is by and against something which is outside of the author.

We are perhaps on the right path to understand Eliot's particular admiration for Dryden as a critic. Dryden, indeed, not only contributed to the formation of a mature English prose and was among the first English writers to make use of a "conversational style" of which Eliot is perhaps the most successful recent exponent but he also represents, in Eliot's opinion, a fruitful example of sanity in criticism: "A great merit of Dryden as a critic and as a critical influence is that he never transgresses the line beyond which the criticisms of the poetry become something else. In the happy age it did not occur to him to enquire what poetry was for, how it affected the nerves of the listeners, how it sublimated the wishes of the poet, whom it should satisfy, and all the other questions which really have nothing to do with poetry as poetry."[33]

32. "The Intentional Fallacy," *Sewanee Review,* LIV (Summer, 1946).
33. *John Dryden, The Poet, The Dramatist, The Critic,* pp. 64–65.

II

ELIOT'S conceptions of art and of the function of the literary critic have of course not been immune from criticism. Edmund Wilson, for instance, accuses Eliot of pedantry and futile aestheticism.[1] While praising Eliot's demand for a more scientific study of aesthetic values, Wilson blames him for what he calls "the impossible attempt to make aesthetic values independent of all the other values." Norman Foerster, who places Eliot in the same category with such more recent critics as J. C. Ransom and Cleanth Brooks, accuses him of limiting our conception of literature and of going to the other extreme of didactic criticism.[2] A more violent and also more superficial critic, Louis Grudin, complains about Eliot's "impulsive dogma" and "dialectical irresponsibility" and censures him for sharing with Paul Valéry the belief in an opposition between two kinds of knowledge.[3]

It is certain that Eliot has always been conscious of the difference between aesthetic values and other values. But as we shall see, he has also been fully aware of the difficulties in making neat distinctions when it came to practical criticism. Edmund Wilson's remark is valid only in so far as it is possible to establish Eliot's basic theoretical position. As we have seen, this basic position does involve the attempt to make aesthetic values independent of other values. Unfortunately—or perhaps fortunately—Eliot has found it extremely difficult, if not impossible, to remain entirely consistent with his critical theories. It was all right, theoretically, to proclaim that aesthetic pleasure does not depend on any particular view of life. In practice Eliot was bound to discover that the question was not quite so easy. The stumbling block—one which has not ceased to torment the critics—was the problem of "belief." "What is the relation of the beauty (the goodness, the perfection) of a poem to the truth or falsity of what it seems to assert?"[4] It is in these words that Cleanth Brooks has summed up the problem in a recent book.

1. See Wilson's chapter on T. S. Eliot in *Axel's Castle*, pp. 93–131.
2. See Foerster's essay "The Esthetic Judgement and the Ethical Judgement," *The Intent of the Critic*, D. A. Stauffer, ed. Foerster's argument for a double standard in literary criticism is very similar to Professor Frederick Pottle's position in *The Idiom of Poetry*.
3. See Louis Grudin's short book *Mr. Eliot among the Nightingales*, pp. 4–9. Grudin discusses in particular Eliot's essay "Poetry and Propaganda."
4. Cleanth Brooks, *The Well Wrought Urn*, p. 140.

The problem of belief in literature began to vex Eliot as early as 1916. He tried to dispose of it then but discovered thereafter that it would arise again and that the matter was not to be settled by merely waving it aside. It was a pressing problem, one that imperiled Eliot's most basic assumptions. But Eliot, instead of evading the issue, faced it with courage, even at the risk of endangering his own theories. That by his very courage and open-mindedness he did more than endanger his theories, I hope to prove in my discussion of a number of important essays covering the period from 1916 to 1941. For a long time Eliot was unwilling to come to rest with any single answer. It is very doubtful whether even today Eliot has found a satisfactory solution. But though he consciously contradicted himself on various occasions, it is very revealing to follow a progression of thought which has led him further and further astray from his theoretical position. This progression will become apparent in considering seven essays: "Theism and Humanism," a book review written in 1916; "Shakespeare and the Stoicism of Seneca," written in 1927 and published again in the *Selected Essays;* the important essay on Dante, published in 1929; "Poetry and Propaganda," which appeared in 1930; the chapter on Shelley and Keats in *The Use of Poetry and the Use of Criticism,* a series of lectures delivered at Harvard University in the winter of 1932–33; "Religion and Literature," which appeared in England in 1935; and finally, Eliot's introductory essay to his *A Choice of Kipling's Verse* in 1941.

At this point, however, and before entering into a closer examination of these essays, it is perhaps useful to point out that there is a difference between the problem of belief and the problem of meaning in poetry. The distinction must be made, not so much because it may not be obvious to the reader as to show that Eliot did not confuse the issues. It was Mallarmé who, echoing Verlaine's *Art Poétique,* believed that music and poetry could become identical. Although Eliot, both as a critic and as a practicing craftsman, has always been interested in the music of poetry, he has never admitted this dangerous identity between verse and music. Eliot's theory that a process of interpretation and abstraction may distort the poem does not divorce the poem from the realm of meanings: "Words are perhaps the hardest material of art: for they must be used to express both visual beauty and beauty of sound, as well as communicating a grammatical statement."[5] In a later essay Eliot was even more explicit, saying that "the music of poetry is not

5. *Ezra Pound, His Metric and Poetry,* p. 14.

something which exists apart from the meaning. Otherwise, we could have poetry of great musical beauty which made no sense, and I have never come across such poetry."[6] The problem of belief in poetry is not whether we must understand the meanings of the poet (for indeed, we must) but whether we are bound to accept temporarily or adopt permanently the ideas of the poet in order to appreciate his art.

As we turn back now to 1916 and to Eliot's essay "Theism and Humanism,"[7] we find that it is precisely this question which already preoccupies him. *Theism and Humanism* is in fact the title of a book by A. J. Balfour which Eliot chose to discuss, one suspects, mainly to express his own views. In this book, Balfour raises the problem of the unaccountability by science of the notions of "good," "truth," and "beauty." Science, Balfour asserts, merely observes phenomena but is unable to explain the existence of values. Balfour, who believes that only theism—that is, the trust in a conscious purpose or design in the universe—can explain their existence, thus raises the problem of the incongruity between our feelings of beauty and any materialistic account of their origin. Eliot, who at that time was far more interested in art than in ethical problems, immediately transposed the issue into the realm of aesthetics. "I fail," he wrote, "to find any such incongruity in art." He is quite willing to agree with Balfour that the enjoyment of beauty is not altogether independent of our world outlook, but he refuses to admit that aesthetic "rapture" (the word is Eliot's) is in any way dependent on any particular theory about the world and its origins. Eliot goes on to remark somewhat gratuitously that most lovers of art probably never have had any explicit philosophy of life at all. Moreover, he claims to see no reason why any man's enjoyment of art should be atrophied by a naturalistic philosophy or stimulated by a theistic one: "No philosophy can force us not to feel or value at all."

We should remember that this was written in 1916 and that Eliot was then only at the beginning of his career as a critic. He had in fact not yet produced a single important essay, and his ideas were only beginning to crystallize. But this book review, in spite of its rather highhanded and superficial manner of dealing with a crucial problem, does at least provide a temporary answer: "So far as we can distinguish the enjoyment of art from our theory about it, there is no reason why the Naturalist and the Theist should not be equally sensitive; when

6. "The Music of Poetry," p. 13.

7. A review of *Theism and Humanism* by the Rt. Hon. A. J. Balfour. *International Journal of Ethics,* XXVI (Jan., 1916).

they value different things they will be valuing on grounds not purely aesthetic." Eliot's argument is that art is a universal language, springing from the emotions and appealing to the emotions, and therefore to be equally appreciated by equally sensitive human beings regardless of any disagreement between the "thoughts" of the artist and the "thoughts" of the public. Theory and belief, according to this position, are outside the realm of aesthetic values. The statement makes allowance, however, for different degrees of appreciation according to the point of view of the reader. Some readers may be bothered by a theory or the absence of one in a literary work. But Eliot insists that when a theory robs art of a value, this value is never an aesthetic one; it robs it perhaps of a belief that gave us pleasure, but if that is the case, we are more attached to the belief than we are to the appreciation of art. What exactly does Eliot mean? To give some examples, imagine an astrologer's disappointment at Milton's conception of astrology in *Paradise Lost* or the irritation of some narrow-minded theologian at the use of pagan mythology in Christian literature. It is obvious, of course, that in "Theism and Humanism" Eliot oversimplifies the issue by too neat a compartmentalization of different categories of values. This position, however, is entirely consistent with Eliot's assertion in "Tradition and the Individual Talent" that "the effect of a work of art upon the person who enjoys it is an experience different in kind from any experience not of art."[8] Balfour's book in 1916 merely suggested to Eliot the problem of belief. As yet he did not see the problem in all its complexity. But the book made enough of an impression on Eliot to convince him that any aesthetico-ethical standard in criticism constituted a grave danger to the impersonal theory of poetry which he was at that time elaborating. This explains perhaps why, in his youthful ardor, he was all too eager to dismiss the problem of belief in rather a dogmatic fashion.

That such an attitude could only postpone the problem soon became apparent to Eliot. In 1926, only six years after the publication of *The Sacred Wood,* he was already willing to make compromises. I refer to an editorial article in the *Criterion* in which Eliot concedes that it is impossible to define the frontiers or limit the context of literature: "Even the purest literature is alimented from non-literary sources, and has non-literary consequences. Pure literature is a chimera of sensation; admit the vestige of an idea and it is already transformed."[9] What

8. For a discussion of this quotation, see Pt. I of this essay.
9. "The Idea of a Literary Review," *Criterion,* IV (Jan., 1926).

Eliot implies here is that the critic, in judging literature intrinsically, cannot wholly neglect its effect and its causality. Words do point to facts or experiences and hence to ideas and concepts. One does not quite see how Eliot hopes to reconcile such a judgment of the intrinsic values of a literary work with a consideration of intent or effect. Eliot does not make the point very clear. What is significant, however, is that although this procedure would depart from his own notion of the proper function of the literary critic, Eliot still draws a sharp distinction between what is intrinsic and what is extrinsic to the work of art. These "non-literary" elements are only "sources" or "consequences." The inside of the work of art still remains protected from intrusions from the outside.

This editorial article has long been forgotten. It was probably never meant to be an important piece of writing. But the compromise is noteworthy. It was written only three years after *The Function of Criticism,* and yet one would hardly believe that the same man was the author of the two essays. If one considers, moreover, that these words were written by Eliot without any apparent provocation, the compromise becomes even more significant. It clearly shows that Eliot was not altogether satisfied with his impersonal theory of poetry. The entire period between 1920 and 1930 might in fact aptly be called a period of faith and doubt: faith in the possibility of theoretical solutions of the problems of the critic, and doubts about their practical applicability. During those years, we can observe Eliot wavering back and forth, hesitating about the very possibility of having any critical dogmas, frequently contradicting himself, unwilling to come to rest with any solution, but unwilling to give up the struggle. The problem of belief was there like a gadfly to torment him.

The editorial article for the *Criterion* must still have been on Eliot's mind a year later when he composed his well-known essay on "Shakespeare and the Stoicism of Seneca."[10] The title of this essay might very well have been "Thought in Art," for that, more than Shakespeare or Seneca, is what Eliot is concerned with. Eliot quotes a passage from Wyndham Lewis' *The Lion and the Fox,* in which the latter maintains that with the exception of Chapman, Shakespeare was the only "thinker" among the Elizabethan dramatists. What bothers Eliot is not that Lewis has forgotten Ben Jonson and Marlowe. It is, as he says, the

10. This essay, written in 1927, was reprinted in the *Selected Essays* (1932).

general notion of "thinking" in art that he wishes to challenge. To begin with, what is the "thought" of the poet? Eliot agrees that we are accustomed to refer to some poets as thinkers and to others as non-thinkers. Lucretius is an example of the former, Tennyson of the latter. But, says Eliot, what distinguishes such poets is not a difference in the quality of the thoughts but in the quality of the emotions: "The poet who thinks is merely the poet who can express the emotional equivalent of thought. But he is not necessarily interested in the thought itself. We talk as if thought was precise and emotion was vague. In reality there is precise emotion and there is vague emotion. To express precise emotion requires as great intellectual power as to express precise thought." The first step in Eliot's argument against Lewis' notion of thinking is to make a distinction between thought and intellectual power. Thought usually exists to some purpose. Precise emotion, on the other hand, may have no purpose but still requires intellectual power. In a much earlier essay Eliot had already expressed his firm conviction that feeling was also an intellectual product.[11] As to the statement that the poet who "thinks" merely expresses the "emotional equivalent of thought"—it reflects a pet theory of Eliot about the fusion of thought and feeling. Was it not he who claimed (very poetically) that the great achievement of the poet was to make us "feel thought" as immediately as the odor of a rose? One of the qualities for which Eliot praises Donne's poetry is its "direct sensuous apprehension of thought, or a re-creation of thought into feeling."[12]

These remarks require some elucidation since they are related to Eliot's conception of the creative process as well as to his conception of the place and function of abstract thought in poetry. First, as to the creative process, Eliot believes that this is to a large extent spontaneous. The mind is a reservoir of innumerable feelings, phrases, and images which may compound at almost any time. But it is not the component parts that count: the greatness of a work of art rests in what Eliot calls "the intensity of the artistic process."[13] As we have already seen in discussing "Tradition and the Individual Talent," it is not the personality but his value as a *medium* that distinguishes the great poet. The feelings of the poet are of value only in so far as they enter into this painful act of depersonalization which is the creation of art. Ants Oras,

11. See "Prose and Verse," *The Chapbook*, 22 (Apr., 1921).
12. "The Metaphysical Poets," *Times Literary Supplement*, 1031 (Oct., 1921); reprinted in the *Selected Essays*.
13. "Tradition and the Individual Talent."

in his essay on the critical ideas of Eliot, has very aptly shown how Eliot conceives of the various stages of the creative process.[14] The first stage, extending over an indefinite period, is the gradual and subterranean accumulation of experience (feelings, phrases, images) in the unconscious well of the poet's memory. The second stage, which may run parallel with this period of accumulation, is a period of experimentation with different techniques. The third and last stage is the moment of spontaneous creation, which can be achieved only if the preparatory work of the second stage has been accomplished. Although Eliot shares many views with the Imagist poets (the passion for precision, the fear of abstractions), he believes that poetry should be expressive of far more than momentary moods.

This oversimplified account of Eliot's conception of the creative process will help us to show what place he assigns to abstract thought in poetry. According to Eliot, the function of poetry is to express an emotion. Yet Eliot holds that an intellectual experience can be a preliminary stage. What he means is that abstract thought, no less than feelings, phrases, and images, can become material for poetry *provided that it is digested and transformed into an emotion.* Art must never become a vehicle for the expression of personal beliefs. Eliot insists on this point: the abstract thought is of value only if it creates an emotion in the poet. This is what Eliot implies when he asks the artist to find an emotional equivalent of thought and to give us its "direct sensuous apprehension." The ideas of the poet—if any—must be *felt* by the reader. And the only way thought can be expressed emotionally in a work of art is through the use of an *objective correlative*: ". . . a set of objects, a situation, a chain of events which shall be the formula of that *particular* emotion; such that when the external facts, which must terminate in sensory experience, are given the emotion is immediately evoked."[15]

Abstract thought, then, is only instrumental in the creation of art. Eliot is—as always—very careful to distinguish between the poet and the poem; between what may be beneficent to the poet as a man and what may do him harm as an artist. Undigested metaphysical speculations can only be harmful to the work of art. Coleridge is a case in point, and Eliot did not fail to observe it. At the stage where beliefs or thoughts may enter into a work of art, the artist should no longer be conscious of them as being held. How seriously Eliot insists on this

14. Ants Oras, *The Critical Ideas of T. S. Eliot.*
15. "Hamlet and his Problems," *Athenaeum,* 4665 (Sept., 1919); reprinted in the *Selected Essays.*

fusion of thought and feeling is evidenced by his somewhat surprising remark in a Harvard lecture that a period of revolution is never favorable to art "since it puts pressure upon the poet, both direct and indirect, to make him overconscious of his beliefs as *held*."[16]

These considerations have led Eliot to the dubious notion that an artist ought not to indulge in original mental speculations lest his moral and intellectual fervor be prejudicial to his task as a creative artist. The conviction that an artist works under the most favorable conditions when his ideas fit into a framework of accepted beliefs coincides with Eliot's more general views about orthodoxy and tradition and partly explains them. According to Eliot, such a framework is valuable because it has a better chance of sinking into the subconscious levels of the artist's mind and hence is probably more beneficent than any personal dynamic creed, or creed in the process of formation. Eliot's theory is that the artist who is simultaneously a thinker will not be able to fuse his thoughts with his feelings.

We may now return to "Shakespeare and the Stoicism of Seneca" with a somewhat better understanding of what Eliot means when he writes that the poet who "thinks" is merely the poet who has found the "emotional equivalent of thought." It is quite clear what Eliot is driving at: he endeavors to eliminate from literary criticism any value judgments of thought content. If the literary critic could accomplish his task by merely judging whether the emotions expressed are precise emotions or not, that would indeed be a simple solution of the problem of belief. Eliot may have been a little worried about the concessions he had made in his editorial article in the *Criterion* and may now have been trying to attenuate them. In order to palliate the difficulty, he implied that the thinking poet need not be a thinker at all.

There was, however, another difficulty. Even if a thinking poet need not be interested in the thoughts themselves and even if whatever thoughts there were originally had been used by the poet merely as material to be subsequently transformed into an emotion, Eliot still had to face the fact that much literature seems to convey a certain view of life. This is certainly true of all great literature. Aeschylus, Dante,

---

16. *The Use of Poetry and the Use of Criticism*, p. 129. Superficially, the remark seems borne out by history; neither the Puritan interlude in England nor the Revolution and Napoleonic wars in France nor the Communist regime in Russia nor the National-Socialist system in Germany have produced any great literature. This, however, may be due mostly to censorship. After all, the Spanish Civil War did stimulate a Malraux and a Hemingway just as the French resistance movement stimulated Sartre, Camus, and Aragon.

Shakespeare, Racine—all make us feel that they are aware of a center of moral and intellectual values. Eliot grants that. Indeed, all great literature seems to imply a view of life which the reader attempts to translate into intellectual terms. But Eliot argues that this view of life is merely an illusion. We are deluded for the simple reason that "every precise emotion tends towards intellectual formulation."

For the second time Eliot calls the "precise emotions" to his rescue. One has the impression that Eliot's argument comes dangerously close to sophistry. For what, in fact, does he say? There is "thought" at the beginning and there is an "intellectual formulation" at the end; but the poem, standing in between, has somehow miraculously escaped from containing any thoughts whatsoever. The aim of this somewhat specious reasoning is clear. Eliot wishes to establish the theoretical innocence of the work of art. We can see how this would reconcile the problem of intellectual beliefs in art with Eliot's impersonal theory of poetry. According to this theory, the work of art is to be judged intrinsically, with reference neither to intent nor to effect. If the thoughts exist only as material used by the poet or as intellectual formulations in the reader's mind, it follows that no consideration of moral or intellectual values must enter into the judgment of the work of art itself.

The argument, however, is not very convincing. How does the work of art escape from containing any thoughts? By what strange coincidence is there usually a strong resemblance between the ideas which the poet used and the ideas which the reader apprehends? And what prevents the artist from also being an original thinker? Are there not examples in Milton, Goethe, Dostoevski, and—more recently—Jean-Paul Sartre? Eliot seems to imply that the only original thinking is done by professional philosophers (who influence the artists) and the university professors (who misinterpret them).

In "Shakespeare and the Stoicism of Seneca," Eliot attempts to convince the reader that he should not judge a work of art in terms of thought content. To support his argument, he gives the example of Dante and Shakespeare. The *Divina Commedia* seems to contain a much more coherent philosophy than does any of Shakespeare's plays. But does that prove that Dante is a greater poet than Shakespeare? Eliot's answer, of course, is no. Eliot's argument is that the artist reflects emotionally the views of his particular time. Dante, living in the thirteenth century, had a coherent system of thought behind him and hence his poetry reflects an orderly system. Shakespeare, who lived at the end of the sixteenth century, at a time when England's air was pregnant with contradictory influences, reflects a chaotic world. But neither Dante nor Shakespeare is responsible for any system of thought. They merely made use of thoughts poetically. "The great poet, in writing himself, writes his time." One somehow has the uncomfortable feeling that Eliot would even go so far as to say that the less a poet thinks, the better he is as a poet. We have this paradoxical statement: "If Shakespeare had written according to a better philosophy, he would have written worse poetry; it was his business to express the greatest emotional intensity of his time, based on whatever his time happened to think."

Several objections could be raised. In the first place, why assume that a better philosophy, if it had been possible for Shakespeare, would have spoiled Shakespeare's plays? This is idle speculation since such plays were never written. Why not rather say that *less* philosophy would have spoiled them? Certainly *King Lear* and *Macbeth* are not less "philosophi- cal" than *Romeo and Juliet* and the *Merchant of Venice*. Secondly—and this objection is more serious—one feels that the comparison of Shake- speare with Dante is not an altogether happy one. After all, Shakespeare was not only a poet; he was also a dramatist. And Dante was not just any poet, but an epic poet. Their functions were not exactly alike. The playwright, in order to be successful, must be objective. His characters must live an independent life. They have a right to self-expression. Moreover, the very nature of drama is to present a conflict. Hence, the "chaos" to which Eliot refers cannot altogether be attributed to the Elizabethan period. An epic poem, on the other hand, implies a cosmic outlook, an organized outlook. The epic needs heroes but only in so far as they are representative of a unified world view. And if we admit this distinction, why believe that a better philosophy would spoil any work of art? Is it just a coincidence that neither Byron nor Shelley nor Tennyson could be successful epic poets? Is it merely a coincidence that the greatest tragedies from the *Book of Job* down to the plays of O'Neill and Paul Claudel deal with the gravest issues that confront mankind?

How little Eliot himself was convinced by the central argument of "Shakespeare and the Stoicism of Seneca" is evidenced in another essay written two years later. In November, 1929, he published "Experiment in Criticism"[17] in which he again emphasized his opinion that the lit- erary critic is not a substitute for the moralist or the theologian. But

17. *The Bookman*, LXX (Nov., 1929).

although he firmly maintains this distinction, Eliot admits that "if we should exclude from literary criticism all but purely literary considerations, there would not only be very little to talk about, but actually we should be left without even 'literary appreciation.'" The pendulum has swung back. Coming only six years after "The Function of Criticism" and barely two years after "Shakespeare and the Stoicism of Seneca," this is quite a remarkable statement. We are as far removed as ever from any possible reconciliation of the problem of belief with the impersonal theory of poetry.

It was in the same year, 1929, that Eliot published his well-known study on Dante.[18] This essay actually represents Eliot's first capital encounter with the problem of belief. For the first time the problem is faced squarely, and if only for this reason the essay is crucial for any understanding of the evolution of Eliot's thought.

Eliot had long been interested in Dante. He even admitted liking him long before achieving any degree of fluency in the Italian language. Also, any study of Eliot's poetry will reveal how much he owes to the *Divina Commedia*. Even such an early poem as the *Love Song of Alfred J. Prufrock* (1917) bears as an epigraph lines from the *Inferno*. F. O. Mathiessen has justly observed that Eliot's feeling for Dante throws considerable light on the very qualities Eliot most values in poetry: craftsmanship, precision of diction, and clear visual images.[19] In his essay on Dante, Eliot calls him the most universal poet ever to write in any modern language and sets his work up as an example of "economy" to the new generations of poets. And yet, although he considers him a most universal and accessible poet, Eliot admits that many modern readers might be rebuffed by Dante's poetry because of its framework of medieval theology.

Eliot raises two questions: (1) Is a previous knowledge of the medieval world essential to appreciate Dante? (2) Is the theological framework of Dante's work irrelevant? In answer to these questions, Eliot admits that a Catholic is probably best equipped to approach Dante and that eventually an adequate background of history, philosophy, and theology is necessary for a full appreciation. Indeed the framework, being functional, cannot be separated from the poetry. At this point, however, Eliot makes a very pertinent distinction: "My point is that you cannot afford to *ignore* Dante's philosophical and theological be-

18. Reprinted in the *Selected Essays*.
19. See F. O. Mathiessen, *op. cit.,* p. 11.

liefs, or to skip the passages which express them most clearly; but that on the other hand you are not called upon to believe them yourself." In other words, the reader must understand the nature of the author's beliefs but need not share them. Consequently, Eliot does admit here that the work of art may contain intellectual and moral beliefs. The reader must be aware of them. But whether or not he shares them has no bearing on his capacity for enjoying the work. Eliot draws a distinction between philosophical *belief* and poetic *assent*. The position taken by Eliot is reminiscent of I. A. Richards' statement that "the beliefs in the arts are . . . provisional acceptances,"[20] which itself is an echo of Coleridge's description of poetic faith, a "willing suspension of disbelief."[21] Eliot amends Coleridge's formula, however, by saying that in fact the reader must suspend both belief and disbelief. He must merely "understand." And for such understanding the Catholic is obviously better equipped, not because he himself has faith but because of previous instruction: "That is the advantage of a coherent traditional system of dogma and morals like the Catholic: it stands apart, for *understanding and assent even without belief. . .* "[22] To sum up: in the case of Dante, Eliot finds it impossible to discard the ideological content. But Eliot maintains that our agreement or disagreement with this content bears no relation to the beauty or perfection of the work of art. Eliot admits that the ideology has a place inside the work of art, but he refuses to allow any judgment of the truth or falsity of this content to influence the appreciation of the art value.

The objections that might be raised Eliot himself has raised in a note to section II of his essay on Dante. It is clear from that note that Eliot still adheres to his impersonal theory of poetry. But on the other hand, it is clear also that he is fully aware that the assumptions implied in this theory need not be accepted by everyone. He concedes that the question may be raised whether literature exists at all in the sense in which he believes that it exists. But "*if* there is 'literature,' *if* there is 'poetry,' then it must be possible to have full literary or poetic appreciation without sharing the beliefs of the poet."

Eliot weakens his case considerably, however, when—in keeping with his inveterate habit of making subtle distinctions—he proceeds to distinguish between the poet's beliefs as a man and his beliefs as a poet—adding, somewhat surprisingly, that the reader must neverthe-

---

20. I. A. Richards, *op. cit.*, p. 278.
21. Coleridge, *Biographia Literaria*, chap. xiv.
22. Italics mine.

less accept the fact that the poet "means what he says." If we learned that *De Rerum Natura* was a Latin exercise which Dante had composed as a relaxation and published under the name of one Lucretius, would that really mutilate our capacity for enjoying the *Divina Commedia*? Eliot believes that it would. But why? Was it not Eliot himself who maintained that a work of art has an existence independent of its author? Why then bring in such distinctions? Suddenly Eliot seems to have shifted his grounds, now emphasizing the relation of the man to his work.

Eliot hastens to add that he is aware of the possible ambiguity of the word "understand." He still maintains that it is possible to have full poetic appreciation without believing what the poet believed. If one denies this, one will have to admit that there is very little poetry indeed that any single reader can appreciate. Eliot aptly remarks that, carried to an extreme, such a denial implies that all appreciation of poetry is eventually dependent on one's individual philosophy. On the other hand, Eliot agrees that "it is possible, and sometimes necessary, to argue that full understanding *must* terminate in belief."

Consequently, Eliot candidly admits that his own theory, if also carried to an extreme, becomes itself a heresy. He even confesses that personally he cannot, at least in practice, wholly separate his poetic appreciation from his personal beliefs. "Actually," Eliot finds, "one probably has more pleasure in the poetry when one shares the beliefs of the poet." The use of the word "more" indicates that Eliot has in mind several degrees of appreciation, the highest of which is to be reached only when the reader can also give his assent to the thought content of a literary work.

Only four paragraphs earlier, however, Eliot has upheld quite a different opinion: "I deny in short that the reader must share the beliefs of the poet in order to enjoy the poetry fully." If the word "fully" can be taken to refer to the highest degree of appreciation, it becomes apparent that the entire note is a masterpiece of contradictions.

The final impression one gathers from reading this note is that Eliot, in spite of his heroic devotion to his theories, is very much embarrassed by the difficulties inhering in what Edmund Wilson calls "the impossible attempt to make aesthetic values independent of all the other values."[23] To be sure, Eliot points out that there is at least one kind of pleasure in enjoying poetry when one does not share the beliefs of the

23. See p. 17, n. 9, "The Idea of a Literary Review."

poet—a pleasure somewhat analogous to the satisfaction we have in mastering other men's philosophical systems even though we do not agree with them. What Eliot fails to notice, however, is that this kind of pleasure is no longer with the object but with the mental process. And the entire note ends with an admission of defeat: "It would appear that 'literary appreciation' is an abstraction, and pure poetry a phantom; and that both in creation and enjoyment much always enters which is, from the point of view of 'Art,' irrelevant."

In a sense, it is regrettable that Eliot should have appended this note to his essay on Dante. Somehow the argument has carried him from one extreme to another. His remarks on poetry and belief in the essay on Dante are, of course, debatable. But at least they represent a definite point of view and are, moreover, consistent with Eliot's theoretical position as a critic. The concessions made in the note (vague as they are) not only weaken his case but constitute a serious symptom of indecision. It is true that Eliot wished merely to make clear some of the inherent difficulties of his theory. But by so doing he admitted the possibility of another extreme (". . . one probably has more pleasure in the poetry when one shares the beliefs of the poet.") to which even the most determined opponents of the impersonal theory of poetry might not wish to subscribe.

In our previous consideration of the essay on "Shakespeare and the Stoicism of Seneca," we have seen that Eliot maintained that it was the business of the poet to express the greatest emotional intensity of his time, based on whatever his time happened to think. In other words, he then denied that a literary artist, merely because his work seems to convey a definite view of life, need necessarily have done any original thinking on his own.

Three years later, in 1930, Eliot again returned to this problem of thought in art. He had come upon a passage in Whitehead's *Science and the Modern World* in which the philosopher, speaking about Shelley and Wordsworth, intimates that the reader can gain from these poets a definite doctrine. As a result, Eliot wrote an essay called "Poetry and Propaganda,"[24] in which he argues that poetry cannot be cited to prove anything; for although the reader is called upon to understand the poet's materials, poetry can at best give only an aesthetic sanction

---

24. *The Bookman*, LXX (Feb., 1930); reprinted in *Literary Opinion in America*, Morton Dauwen Zabel, ed., pp. 25-38.

to beliefs. According to Eliot, only the imperfect reader takes the poet as a propagandist.

What is remarkable in Eliot's argument, however, is that he now makes a distinction between different types of poets:

There is the philosophic poet like Lucretius and Dante, who accepts one philosophy of life, so to speak, in advance, and who constructs his poem on one idea. There is the poet like Shakespeare, or possibly Sophocles, who accepts current ideas and makes use of them, but in whose work the question of belief is much more baffling and evasive. There is finally another type, of which we might take Goethe as an example, who neither quite accepts a particular view of the whole, nor merely sees views of life to make poetry out of, but who in himself more or less combines the function of the philosopher and poet—or perhaps Blake; poets who have their own ideas and definitely believe them.

Eliot not only admits here that a poet can simultaneously be an original thinker; he also admits that his thoughts may in fact be the very motivating force in the artistic creation. But what is even more important, Eliot in this same essay suddenly begins to concern himself with the relation of the philosophy to the greatness of the poetry. This, in reality, is the very core of the problem of belief.

We remember that on a previous occasion Eliot suggested somewhat paradoxically that if Shakespeare had written according to a better philosophy, he probably would have written worse poetry. In "Poetry and Propaganda," he again maintains that everything depends on the artistic abilities of the poet. Thus, an inferior poet may use a sound philosophy in vain, while another, more gifted, may give great validity to an inferior philosophy. But here follows a truly astonishing statement: "We can hardly doubt that the 'truest' philosophy is the best material for the greatest poet; so that the poet must be rated in the end both by the philosophy he realizes and by the fulness and adequacy of the realization." This statement contains a very important implication, namely that the philosophy expressed is an important criterion for judging the artistic value of a poem. The thought content in the work of art must be judged along with the poetic use that is made of it. Eliot is here beginning to draw a distinction between the philosophy realized and the "fulness and adequacy of the realization" which he would never have admitted in 1916, at the time he reviewed Balfour's book on *Theism and Humanism*.

In his chapter on Shelley and Keats, in *The Use of Poetry and the Use of Criticism*,[25] Eliot is even more explicit. In his attempt to explain his particular aversion to Shelley—an aversion which, one suspects, is partly a reaction against an overenthusiastic adolescent experience—Eliot writes: "When the doctrine, theory, belief or 'view of life' presented in a poem is one which the mind of the reader can accept as coherent, mature, and founded on the facts of experience, it interposes no obstacle to the reader's enjoyment, whether it be one he accept or deny, approve or deprecate. When it is one which the reader rejects as childish or feeble, it may, for a reader of well-developed mind, set up an almost complete check." But this attempt to outflank the problem of belief is not very satisfactory. In fact, Eliot asserts no less than that in one sense the thought content can determine the value of the poem, though in another sense it cannot. It should be noted that Eliot does not qualify as childish and feeble the "fulness and adequacy of the realization" but that he lends these attributes to the "view of life" presented in the poems. In other words, he judges Shelley no longer as a poet but as a thinker at two removes from the criterion of acceptable truth.

This is not merely a slip of the pen. That Eliot was quite conscious of the importance of this chapter is borne out by another statement in which he apparently refers to his impersonal theory of poetry: "I am not sure that this critical eclecticism cannot go too far; that we can judge and enjoy a man's poetry while leaving wholly out of account all things for which he cared deeply, and on behalf of which he turned his poetry to account."

It is hardly an exaggeration to say that Eliot could have written nothing more startling. What is implied in this statement is far more than was ever implied in "Poetry and Propaganda." There Eliot merely pointed out that the philosophy presented in the poem must be taken into consideration by the reader as an important factor for determining the value of the poem. But the philosophy was still seen inside the poem as an integral part of the work of art. In his discussion on Shelley, however, Eliot considers it necessary to take into account the nature of the beliefs as they existed anterior to the creation of the poem. The reader is invited to inquire into all the things for which the author cared deeply. The poem must now also be appraised in terms of the author's personality. The argument has been shifted from the poem to the poet.

Nor was this merely a temporary pronouncement. Indeed, in 1935

25. See pp. 87–102.

Eliot confirmed this unexpected position in somewhat similar terms. In "Religion and Literature"[26] he suggests that literary criticism must be completed by criticism from a definite ethical and theological standpoint: "The 'greatness' of literature cannot be determined solely by literary standards; though we must remember that whether it is literature or not can be determined only by literary standards." And Eliot warns the critic: "If we, as readers, keep our religious and moral convictions in one compartment, and take our reading merely for entertainment, or on a higher plane, for aesthetic pleasure, I would point out that the author, whatever his conscious intentions in writing, in practice recognizes no such distinctions."

It is obvious that by inviting the critic to take into consideration factors which lie outside the work of art as such, Eliot calls for the very method he so strenuously denounced in "Tradition and the Individual Talent." If, in order to assess the artistic value of a poem the critic must also consider the author's personality (". . . all the things for which he cared deeply,") even though the author himself may not have been conscious of the extent to which his personal beliefs have found a place in his work, then criticism inevitably becomes concerned with the intentional aspect of literature. From the moment that a shift is made from the poem to the poet, the entire impersonal theory of poetry collapses.

The fruits of this shift to the personal and intentional aspect of the work of art are to be most clearly observed in Eliot's introductory essay to his *A Choice of Kipling's Verse*.[27] The first striking characteristic of this essay is the repeated use of such words as "intent," "intended," and "intentional." Eliot remarks that "Kipling certainly thought of verse as well as prose as a medium for a public purpose." It is noteworthy that Eliot has nothing to say about this attitude. He presents this merely as a fact and then proceeds to consider purely biographical data as well as the effect of Kipling's verse on his contemporaries. As to Eliot's method of evaluating Kipling's achievement, it consists exclusively in measuring what Kipling set out to achieve against what his contemporaries, or we today, have considered his achievement to be: ". . . we must consider what Kipling was trying to do and what he was not trying to do"—this seems to be the central problem. Kipling's

---

26. V. A. Demant, ed., *Faith That Illuminates*, pp. 29–54; reprinted in *Essays Ancient and Modern*.

27. Published in 1941.

poetry is seen merely as an instrument, and apparently a successful one, since we are told that there is hardly any poem in which Kipling fails to do what he planned. Whether that which he planned was good or bad, whether to succeed in a design is the criterion of a good poet— these are questions which Eliot leaves unanswered.

The essay on Kipling is certainly disconcerting. Perhaps this is partly due to an evident carelessness in composition. One feels somehow that these pages have been produced with too much facility. Certainly we do not find here the clarity, the inquisitiveness, and the insight of Eliot's better writings. As a document, it presents only a meager interest for our inquiry. Nor have I mentioned it in order to cast discredit on Eliot's more recent criticism—although a good case could probably be made tracing a steady decline in the quality and critical acuteness of Eliot's recent prose.

In one respect, however, this essay is significant. Its argument shifts back and forth from intent to effect without any solid standards. It remains a warning sign pointing to the kind of blind alley into which Eliot saw himself forced as a result of a deep confusion. The time has now come to pause and consider the nature of this confusion.

III

IN "Tradition and the Individual Talent," Eliot had formulated a theory calling upon the critic to direct his attention not upon the poet but upon poetry. He there maintained that what counted in art was not the greatness of the emotions expressed but "the intensity of the artistic process." The poem, according to this theory, was not a vehicle for expressing the author's personality nor an instrument for communicating ideas but a product having an autonomous existence and an intrinsic value. This essay, as Eliot himself suggested, laid the foundations of the impersonal theory of poetry.

Simultaneously with the formulation of this theory and beginning as early as 1916, Eliot had also become increasingly aware of the difficulties in limiting criticism to purely literary considerations. The stumbling block, as I have already suggested, was the problem of belief, that is, essentially, the relation of the goodness of the poem to the truth or falsity of what it seems to assert. This struggle to reconcile a very complex problem with his basic theoretical position forms the subject matter of most of the important essays Eliot produced during the twenty years following the publication of "Tradition and the Individual Talent." A progression of thought, frequently tortuous and contradictory, yet nevertheless a very marked progression, carried Eliot from an early denial of any dual standard—aesthetic and ethical—in criticism to the mounting conviction that there exists a definite relation between the greatness of a poem and the nature of the philosophy it expresses.

The fear of any aesthetico-ethical standard in criticism led Eliot to assert that from the point of view of Art only the aesthetic values were to be taken into consideration. Very soon, however, he had to concede that pure literature was only a chimera and that much entered into a work of art which could not be accounted for in purely aesthetic terms. Next, although insisting that the poet was not really a thinker, Eliot agreed that intellectual beliefs expressed in a poem could not be neglected. In his essay on Dante, Eliot maintained that the reader, in order to appreciate the poetry, was not called upon to share but merely to understand the beliefs expressed. Then followed a series of concessions: first, that it was not possible in practice to separate appreciation from belief; secondly, that there existed poets who were simultaneously thinkers; thirdly, that the beliefs expressed stood in a definite relation to the greatness of the poetry; and finally, that the reader, in order fully to judge and appreciate the poetry, could not leave out of account the beliefs and the personality of the author himself.

It is difficult to see why the author's personality had to become involved. Somewhere along the line of Eliot's thought a confusion between two really unrelated problems must have taken place. As we look back at the various essays we have discussed, it becomes apparent that this confusion first manifests itself in the chapter dealing with Shelley in *The Use of Poetry and the Use of Criticism*. Already in our discussion of "Poetry and Propaganda" (1930) we were uncomfortably surprised to read Eliot's classification of various types of poets according to degrees of philosophic originality. It was also in the same essay that we were told that the "truest" philosophy was undoubtedly the best material for the greatest poet. Up to this point, however, the two issues of poet and poem were treated separately.

But in his chapter on Shelley and even more explicitly in "Religion and Literature" (1935), Eliot combines these issues. To consider first what he says on the issue of the aesthetico-ethical standard in criticism, he finally has come to the conclusion that a poem must also be judged from a definite ethical standpoint. The critic is thus called upon to perform a two-step analysis. Whether a poem is a work of art at all can, to be sure, only be determined by literary standards. But in order to ascertain the greatness of the work of art, literary criticism must be completed by an appraisal from a definite ethical standpoint.

This position is far removed indeed from Eliot's early conception of the literary critic as one whose business it was to analyze, compare, and elucidate, but not to pass judgments for worse or better. One may feel, however, in spite of some new difficulties that this position creates, that it is on the whole a sounder conception of the functions of the critic. Thus, in so far as Eliot merely enlarged the realm of jurisdiction of the critic by inviting him to pass judgments on the nature of the thought content, one may even rejoice at some of the inconsistencies of Eliot's arguments. As Eliot himself came to realize, if all but purely literary considerations were excluded from criticism, we should soon be left without any literary appreciation whatsoever.

What is highly disturbing, however, is that in the course of his arguments Eliot has shifted his ground from the work of art back to the author. In the chapter on Shelley, the thread of the one problem has become interwoven with the thread of the other. It is surprising that

Eliot, who had always been so careful to distinguish between the author, the work of art, and the reader should have confused the issues by implying that from the moment that the critic considers the philosophy expressed in the poem he must also take into consideration all of the things for which the author cared deeply. Granted that the philosophy contained in the poem stands in relation to the artistic quality of the poem; granted also that it is not possible in practice to separate poetic composition from the beliefs of the author and poetic appreciation from the beliefs of the readers—it does not follow that the morality of the poem and the morality of its author are one and the same thing.

It is likely that the confusion in Eliot's mind arose from the fact that he was preoccupied with two separate sets of questions simultaneously. There is on the one hand the problem of the work of art, namely whether it contains any moral values, and if so, whether these values stand in any relation to the artistic merits of that work. If there is such a relation, then the critic is justified in taking these values as a standard but only in so far as they have become an integral part of the art product. The other problem is concerned with the author, namely whether he be habitually either an original or a sound thinker, and if he is either, to what extent he has made use of his artistic abilities, consciously or unconsciously, to give expression to his personal beliefs.

These are the two problems, both legitimate in their own context. But here is what happened: on the one hand, Eliot found that the thought content had to be a definite criterion for assessing the over-all merit of a work of art; and on the other hand, he conceded, reluctantly to be sure, that a poet could also be an original thinker and express poetically ideas which he firmly believed. And from these two propositions, Eliot in his discussion of Shelley jumped to the conclusion that literary criticism must be directed also upon what the author as a person believed. What has happened is nothing less than a flagrant repudiation of the dictum set forth in "Tradition and the Individual Talent" that "honest criticism and sensitive appreciation are directed not upon the poet but upon poetry."

The confusion rests not only in the assumption that the morality of the author and the morality of the poem are one and the same thing. An even worse fallacy results from the implied assumption that the author's personal feelings, thoughts, and beliefs—in short, his personality—can be taken as criteria for measuring his artistic achievement. Surely a poet's personal feelings are a motivating force in the artistic creation. But a motivating force is only a cause, not a standard. Should the well-carried-out purpose become a criterion, we should soon find ourselves denying an obvious artistic success on the grounds that it does not correspond to the author's original intention. Carried to an extreme, such a method of criticism might lead to a rejection of *Paradise Lost* on the grounds that it does not really justify the ways of God to men. With respect to intrinsic literary criticism, the problem of whether the poet thinks or does not think is not of such importance after all. Shelley may have been intelligent or unintelligent, profound or superficial, but such considerations make his poetry neither worse nor better. It is quite true, as Mortimer J. Adler observes in his *Art and Prudence,* that the object of imitation for most arts is human action and the moral life. Hence the artist "cannot help but reveal the tenor of his moral judgments."[1] But although a poem could in a way be used as a document to determine the moral soundness of its creator, it does not follow that the moral life and attitudes of the creator can determine the artistic quality of his poem. It is quite obvious "that a man can be good as an artist of a particular sort without being a good man . . ."[2] After having inquired into all the peculiarities of a poet's mind, we are still faced with the task of assessing his poetry as poetry.

Eliot's account of the obstacles he found in Shelley's poetry raises another sort of difficulty. How satisfactory this proposed solution of the problem of belief in the poem really is remains a point still to be settled. As we remember, Eliot had pointed out that the question of belief or disbelief should never even occur to the reader. The passage is important enough to be quoted again: "When the doctrine, theory, belief or 'view of life' presented in a poem is one which the mind of the reader can accept as coherent, mature, and founded on the facts of experience, it interposes no obstacle to the reader's enjoyment, whether it be one he accept or deny, approve or deprecate. When it is one which the reader rejects as childish or feeble, it may, for a reader of well-developed mind, set up an almost complete check."[3] The choice of terms is perhaps unfortunate here. For what precisely is the difference between a view of life which the reader deprecates and a view of life which he rejects as childish or feeble? And how can the reader deny that which he accepts as coherent, mature, and founded on the facts of experience? Had Eliot made it clear that it was Shelley's *presentation* of a view of life which he rejected as childish, the entire passage would

1. Mortimer J. Adler, *Art and Prudence,* p. 444.
2. *Ibid.,* p. 443.
3. See the chapter on Shelley and Keats in *The Use of Poetry and the Use of Criticism.*

be less ambiguous. As it stands, however, the statement appears unfortunately like a dexterous attempt to circumvent the essential question of approval and denial on a philosophic level.

The matter is of course open to debate. Although this is probably one of Eliot's most explicit passages concerning this central problem, it seems open to the most varied interpretations as to the real meaning implied. On the one hand, it may be taken to signify that Eliot decidedly refuses to disregard intellectual standards on behalf of the poets. It may be taken to suggest that if Shelley's argument is foolish, it makes his poetry foolish also. But if Eliot really saw no reason for waiving intellectual standards on behalf of the poets, why did he insert the confusing words ". . . whether it be one he accept or deny, approve or deprecate"—words which certainly tend to dilute this supposed meaning?

It would seem that the explanation offered by Cleanth Brooks in *The Well Wrought Urn* comes closer to a satisfactory solution. It should be remembered that Brooks does not believe that a poem achieves coherence in a system of logically related propositions but rather "in a complex of attitudes dramatically related to each other."[4] As we see, this view comes close to Eliot's own conception of the objective correlative. The poem, according to Brooks, has to be judged in terms of its structural coherence.[5] Eliot himself had maintained in a discussion of the Elizabethan drama that a primary requirement of a work of art is that it be "self-consistent."[6] The maturity of a poem, in Brooks' opinion, rests precisely in its structural realization. "Would not Eliot make his case stronger," asks Brooks in discussing Eliot's difficulties with Shelley, "by frankly developing the principle of dramatic propriety suggested by his statement and by refraining from attempting to extract any proposition from the poem at all?"[7]

Brooks suggests that what had troubled Eliot was the very fact that his belief or disbelief had been aroused: "Certain statements, explicit or implied, because they are not totally assimilated, wrench themselves free from the context, and demand to be judged on ethical or religious grounds."[8]

---

4. *The Well Wrought Urn*, p. 220.
5. The demand that the critic examine and define the poem with regards to structure and texture has also been formulated by J. C. Ransom in "Criticism as Pure Speculation," *The Intent of the Critic*, D. A. Stauffer, ed. (1941), pp. 65–88.
6. See "Four Elizabethan Dramatists," *Criterion*, II (Feb., 1924), pp. 115–123.
7. *The Well Wrought Urn*, p. 228.
8. *Ibid.*, p. 227.

What Brooks demands is a sort of fair play between the poet and the reader. If, on the one hand, the good reader must subordinate his private interests to the total experience, the good poem, on the other hand, should not trouble this discipline of the reader by presenting nonfunctional propositions which would appeal to these private interests. As Eliot himself realized, to enjoy a poem the question of belief or disbelief must not even occur to the reader. What Eliot failed to emphasize, according to Brooks, is that this depends primarily on the nature of the poem. A good poem, one that is structurally coherent and mature, will elude the problem of belief. Thus, if the problem of belief arises at all, it is only as a symptom of an artistic defect, namely a looseness of structure by which certain elements, as Brooks suggests, "are not totally assimilated to a total context."

The solution to the problem of belief offered by Brooks evidently rests on a theory of poetry which, though it enjoys great popularity today, need not be accepted by everyone. Professor Frederick Pottle in *The Idiom of Poetry*[9] has aptly remarked that although the kind of poetry which is free from explicit message or interpretation may respond to our present sensibility, it does not follow that the critical norm of pure poetry is a desirable one for judging works of the past. Brooks' solution, however, is certainly valuable in so far as it helps to clarify an obscure point in Eliot's position or perhaps to carry Eliot's argument a step further toward its logical conclusion.

Eliot himself has been aware of the necessary limitations of all critical theories. After he outgrew his early period of "pontifical solemnity," as he termed it himself, his views became more modest and more tolerant. In his Harvard lectures during the winter of 1932–33, he maintained that critical speculation should be free to follow its own course without being called upon to show immediate results. As the years went on, however, be became increasingly suspicious of any dogmatic theories. That he was convinced that criticism could never be final is surely demonstrated by his own practice as well as by his reiterated demands that "each generation must make its own appraisal of the poetry of the past...."[10] Eliot's notion of tradition should not be confused with rigid conservatism. There is nothing rigid in his view of Western literature. The "ideal order" to which he refers in "Tradition and the Individual Talent" is seen as constantly altered by new works of art. It

9. Professor Pottle's theory of critical relativism calls for a two-standard literary criticism in which the moral criteria alone are permanent and absolute.
10. *The Use of Poetry and the Use of Criticism*, p. 64.

is in a constant flux. Nor is the "tradition" something which the individual merely inherits and jealously protects. He has to obtain it by great personal labor.

> Was du ererbt von deinen Vaetern hast,
> Erwirb es, um es zu besitzen.

The words of Faust serve well to illustrate the kind of dynamic attitude which Eliot expects from each new generation of artists and critics.

In *The Use of Poetry and the Use of Criticism* Eliot has pointed out that the majority of critics can be expected only to repeat the opinions of the last master of criticism until the day a new authority appears to introduce a new order. But Eliot very wisely explains that it is not merely because this new authority has true insight and originality that he can impose on his contemporaries a fresh vision of the existing literary monuments. It is also because his contemporaries as a result of periodical shifts of interest and sensibility require new visions. New assessments, as Eliot points out, are inevitable so long as appreciation of art is an affair of limited and transient human beings:

No generation is interested in Art quite the same way as any other; each generation, like each individual, brings to the contemplation of art its own categories of appreciation, makes its own demands upon art, and has its own uses for art . . . There is for each time, for each artist, a kind of alloy required to make the metal workable into art; and each generation prefers its own alloy to any other. Hence each new master of criticism performs a useful service merely by the fact that his errors are of a different kind from the last; and the longer sequence of critics we have, the greater amount of correction is possible.[11]

11. *The Use of Poetry and the Use of Criticism*, pp. 101–102.

BIBLIOGRAPHY

Many of the essays to which I refer are easily available. They are contained either in *The Sacred Wood,* the *Selected Essays,* or *The Use of Poetry and the Use of Criticism.* Some others, unfortunately, have never been exhumed from the various reviews in which they lie temporarily buried. Donald Gallup's very useful *Bibliographical Check-List of the Writings of T. S. Eliot* has helped me immeasurably in locating a number of these essays, articles, and book reviews in such publications as the *International Journal of Ethics,* the *New Statesman,* the *Egoist,* the *Athenaeum,* and of course the *Criterion* of which Eliot was the editor until shortly before World War II. Some of these essays definitely deserve to be reprinted, and it is to be hoped that some future collection of Eliot's writings will bring them back to light.

Of the critical studies on Eliot that I have found most useful, I would mention Ants Oras' account of *The Critical Ideas of T. S. Eliot,* which is a sound if not always penetrating survey of Eliot's ideas up to 1928, and particularly F. O. Mathiessen's *The Achievement of T. S. Eliot* which, although dealing primarily with Eliot's poetry, nevertheless shows great insight into Eliot's critical thought.

A. BOOKS AND PAMPHLETS BY T. S. ELIOT

Ezra Pound, His Metric and Poetry. Knopf, New York, 1917.
The Sacred Wood. Methuen and Company, London, 1920.
Shakespeare and the Stoicism of Seneca. Oxford University Press, London, 1927.
Dante. Faber and Faber, London, 1929.
Selected Essays 1917–1932. Harcourt, Brace and Company, London, 1932.
John Dryden, The Poet, The Dramatist, The Critic. T. and Elsa Holliday, New York, 1932.
The Use of Poetry and the Use of Criticism. Harvard University Press, 1933.
After Strange Gods. Faber and Faber, London, 1934.
Essays Ancient and Modern. Faber and Faber, London, 1936.
Collected Poems 1909–1935. Harcourt, Brace and Company, New York, 1936.
A Choice of Kipling's Verse. Faber and Faber, London, 1941.
The Music of Poetry. Jackson, Son and Company, Glasgow, 1942.
The Classics and the Man of Letters. Oxford University Press, London, 1943.
Four Quartets. Harcourt, Brace and Company, New York, 1943.
What is a Classic? Faber and Faber, London, 1945.

B. BOOKS AND PAMPHLETS WITH CONTRIBUTIONS FROM T. S. ELIOT

A Brief Introduction to the Method of Paul Valery. R. Cobden-Sanderson, London, 1924.

"Experiment in Criticism," *Tradition and Experiment in Present-Day Literature.* Oxford University Press, London, 1929.

"Baudelaire," introduction to *Intimate Journals* by Baudelaire. The Blackamore Press, New York, 1930.

"The 'Pensées' of Pascal," introduction to *Pensées* by Pascal. J. M. Dent and Sons, New York, 1931.

"Religion and Literature," *Faith That Illuminates.* The Centenary Press, London, 1935.

"In Memoriam," introduction to *Poems of Tennyson.* T. Nelson and Sons, New York, 1936.

"Byron (1778–1824)," *From Anne to Victoria.* Cassell and Company, London, 1937.

"Poetry and Propaganda," *Literary Opinion in America.* Harper and Brothers, New York, 1937.

C. CONTRIBUTIONS BY T. S. ELIOT TO PERIODICALS

"Theism and Humanism," *International Journal of Ethics,* XXVI (Jan., 1916), 284–289.

"An American Critic," *New Statesman,* VII (June, 1916), 284.

"The Ultimate Belief," *International Journal of Ethics,* XXVII (Oct., 1916), 127.

"Classics in English," *Poetry,* IX (Nov., 1916), 101–104.

"Reflections on Vers Libre," *New Statesman,* VIII (March, 1917), 518–519.

"The Borderline of Prose," *New Statesman,* IX (May, 1917), 157–159.

"The Noh and the Image," *Egoist,* IV (Aug., 1917), 102–103.

"Reflections on Contemporary Poetry," *Egoist,* IV (Sept., Oct., Nov., 1917), 118–119, 133–134, 151.

"Studies in Contemporary Criticism," *Egoist,* V (Oct., Nov., Dec., 1918), 113–114, 131–133.

"A Romantic Patrician," *Athenaeum,* 4644 (May, 1919), 265–267.

"Beyle and Balzac," *Athenaeum,* 4648 (May, 1919), 392–398.

"Criticism in England," *Athenaeum,* 4650 (June, 1919), 456–457.

"The Education of Taste," *Athenaeum,* 4652 (June, 1919), 520–521.

"The Method of Mr. Pound," *Athenaeum,* 4669 (Oct., 1919), 1065–1066.

"The Local Flavour," *Athenaeum,* 4676 (Dec., 1919), 1332–1333.

"A Brief Treatise on the Criticism of Poetry," *The Chapbook,* II (March, 1920), 1–10.

"Dante as a 'Spiritual Leader,'" *Athenaeum,* 4692 (April, 1920), 441–442.

"Prose and Verse," *The Chapbook,* 22 (April, 1921), 3–10.

"The Function of a Literary Review," *Criterion,* I (July, 1923), 421.

"The Function of Criticism," *Criterion,* II (Oct., 1923), 31–42.

"Lettre d'Angleterre," *Nouvelle Revue Française,* 122 (Nov., 1923), 619–625.

"Four Elizabethan Dramatists," *Criterion,* II (Feb., 1924), 115–123.

"The Idea of a Literary Review," *Criterion,* IV (Jan., 1926), 1–6.

"Experiment in Criticism," *The Bookman,* LXX (Nov., 1929), 225–233.
"Poetry and Propaganda," *The Bookman,* LXX (Feb., 1930), 595–602.
"Tradition and Orthodoxy," *American Review,* II (March, 1934), 513–528.

D. CRITICAL STUDIES OF T. S. ELIOT'S WORKS: BOOKS AND CHAPTERS IN BOOKS

Church, Richard, "Eliot: a Search for Foundations," *Eight for Immortality.* J. M. Dent and Sons, London, 1941.

Frank, Waldo D., "The Universe of T. S. Eliot," *In the American Jungle.* Farrar and Rinehart, New York, 1937.

Gallup, Donald, *A Bibliographical Check-List of the Writings of T. S. Eliot.* Yale University Library, New Haven, 1947.

Grudin, Louis, *Mr. Eliot among the Nightingales.* L. Drake, Paris, 1932.

Leavis, Frank R., *New Bearings in English Poetry.* Chatto and Windus, London, 1932.

Loggins, Vernon, "Intellectualism and Experiment," *I Hear America.* Thomas Y. Crowell Company, New York, 1937.

Mathiessen, F. O., *The Achievement of T. S. Eliot.* Oxford University Press, New York and London, 1947.

Oras, Ants, *The Critical Ideas of T. S. Eliot.* K. Mathiessen Ltd., Tartu, 1932.

Pound, Ezra, "Mr. Eliot's Solid Merit," *Polite Essays.* Faber and Faber, London, 1937.

Ransom, John C., "T. S. Eliot: the Historical Critic," *The New Criticism.* New Directions, Norfolk, 1941.

Spender, Stephen, *The Destructive Element.* J. Cape, London, 1935.

Wilson, Edmund, *Axel's Castle.* C. Scribner, New York, 1931.

E. CRITICAL STUDIES OF T. S. ELIOT'S WORK: ARTICLES IN PERIODICALS

Collin, W. E., "T. S. Eliot the Critic," *Sewanee Review,* 39 (Oct., 1931), 419–424.

Strong, R., "The Critical Attitude of T. S. Eliot," *London Quarterly Review,* 158 (Oct., 1933), 513–519.

Weiss, T., "T. S. Eliot and the Courtyard Revolution," *Sewanee Review,* 54 (April, 1946), 289–307.

Williamson, H. R., "T. S. Eliot and His Conception of Poetry," *The Bookman,* 79 (March, 1931), 347–350.

F. GENERAL

Adler, Mortimer J., *Art and Prudence.* Longmans, Green and Company, New York, Toronto, 1937.

Brooks, Cleanth, *The Well Wrought Urn*. Reynal and Hitchcock, New York, 1947.

Foerster, Norman, "The Esthetic Judgement and the Ethical Judgement," *The Intent of the Critic*. Princeton University Press, Princeton, 1941.

Joyce, James, *The Portrait of the Artist as a Young Man*. Random House.

Lowes, John L., *The Road to Xanadu*. Houghton Mifflin Company, Boston and New York, 1930.

Maurras, Charles, *Prologue d'un Essai sur la critique*. La Porte Etroite, Paris, 1932.

Pottle, Frederick, *The Idiom of Poetry*. Cornell University Press, Ithaca, 1941.

Ransom, John C., "Criticism as Pure Speculation," *The Intent of the Critic*. Princeton University Press, Princeton, 1941.

Richards, I. A., *Principles of Literary Criticism*. Harcourt, Brace and Company, New York, 1945.

Stauffer, Donald A., "Introduction," *The Intent of the Critic*. Princeton University Press, Princeton, 1941.

Wilson, Edmund, "The Historical Interpretation of Literature," *The Intent of the Critic*. Princeton University Press, Princeton, 1941.

UNDERGRADUATE PRIZE ESSAYS